two thousand and twenty years

an anthology

KRISTIAN JEFF CORTEZ AGUSTIN

...and misery
...that it tears more...
...then the heart...
...something so delic...
...that makes too qui...
...der a storm of te...
...more, a well...
...write

PUBLISHED BY

UNIVERSE AND WORDS
LONDON

TWO HUNDRED AND TWENTY YEARS
AN ANTHOLOGY
Copyright © 2020 Kristian Jeff Cortez Agustin
The UK Copyright Service Reg No 284738585
ISBN 978 0 9574658 2 4

A catalogue record for this book is available from the British Library.

Published in London, England.

PROLOGUE

To deter even the slightest thought of eternity
and what comes after this aching body and soul
I must write.

For I distrust my eyes:

PART I
PANDEMONIUM

What is, we often ask, real?

Is it the slightest thought that moves and shakes the ground or the tangible matter that lays still and fills the empty space?

I roll myself out of bed, head to the kitchen and set the kettle to boil. Minutes pass.

What once was thought of as fiction is already coming for us. Perhaps 'dystopian' is code word for today's conditions of existence which many bygone writers had anticipated. Moreso narrowly predicted. In fact, many crucial, devastating events are underreported, especially those that occur far from the very centre. The seemingly placid humdrum of our everyday life is an illusion.

We might have been contributing to the dystopic blueprint all along. And it only takes one mastermind to pick something up and implement what's written. By the book.

Yet another unfinished chapter lingers in my dim-lit room. Even before evening fell, I left half of the lights on so I could find my way through the accumulation of digital ticks, clutter of missing footage, and growing virtual dog ears.

As if they were meant to eavesdrop whenever I curse his plan.

Haven't you heard?

The kettle whistles.

CAUGHT IN THE CROSSFIRE

What if it explodes?

> It would then be over before we know it
> we are as good as gone
> this thing, we can never outrun

Short limbs, short memories, all that we are
every time we try to seize control, lose control

> We spark, short fuse

And in our short-sightedness, we're no different
from the one who turns a blind, evil eye
no matter how he can never unsee
his own consciousness

> His own conscience

Whose appetite is as mighty as the mountain?
Whose underbelly is as robust as the forest?
Whose hunger is as abysmal as hell?

> I know his face
> his lecherous countenance
> dare never speak of his ungodly name
> for when I mouth his existence, his words
> taste of poison, reek of illusion
> and the bitter truth of lies.

What if it explodes?

> From a single pinprick in the midst of the void
> faster than heartbeats rushing into the wild
> spread tongues of fire savouring its kill
> there's no chance of escaping.

DAY 17, GRIT

Leave now, before they catch you
ignore any stranger who stops you
conceal your face
lower your voice
run like mad

> Each time you drive yourself mad
> through miles of endless winding roads
> cutting across rocks and mountains
> curling around unnamed forests
> you are the reason I am lost.

They are closing in unless you flee the hell they are

> Each time you drive yourself mad
> through miles of endless winding roads
> cutting across columns and skyscrapers
> turning around posts and stations
> I am the reason you are lost.

HEAT

Minute by minute rounding herds and herbs
scaling great mounds of timber
two lovers intimate their narrowest escape
from the bitter brink of annihilation
twenty years
two decades
one score.

Recall, one said, how we trembled in terror

>   no, not terrified only teetering
>   said the other

Yes, how we teased over every edge
at the very verge of the millennia:

Suppose we lose our names, or fail to write

>   our names for every single thing

Yes, and we are forced to start ever again

>   or worst, never again
>   said the other

Suppose we lose track of time

>   or time loses its sense and steam

Yes, like a derailed omnibus of matter

>   or worst, everything that matters

Matter.

Every matter.

Will we still find each other amongst the gaps in the cloud?

        did you mean:
        digital screens and everything that pries
        in between?

Will you stop second-guessing my thoughts?

        or seconding every guest of thought
        each person who knocks you unconscious
        knock, knock, is there anybody?

        Why not let me be your shadow
        I cast my spell upon the ground, kiss your feet
        upon the sturdy tree trunks, hold your hand
        upon the rain, cover your eyes!

Rain as dry as scathing sand
bristling at your eyelids, balls of fire!
Turn around, run roundabout!

        Find your way back, save your body, self

How dare I leave you alone with no body?

        Leave now, never return your gaze
        fire is grazing, ground is fraying
        pray, let me burn amongst the sea of souls
        the sea of sins fuelling the wild,
        pouring, purging,
        timid beasts, trepid sods, torpid skies
        thrusting into the stratosphere

Enrage my heart with belting fury
flaming ashes, dust to dust
shove their mouths with boulders of bodies
until the mountain has had its fill
until the forest has had its meal
stench clawing through the pulsating rubble
not even a single lick of life left
feathers, scales, wings, snouts, paws, tongues
fangs, molars, throngs of stillborn savages
gallons of nucleic acid belch death threats
and morbid desires

Remember our impassioned plea falling on ears
unhearing, unnerving, unturning blind eyes
watching us from a distance
rebelling and revelling
bless our youth!

Bless our youth, our bones unbreaking
bending our will to suit each twist and turn
delighting in the ecstatic thrust of desire
setting our obsession on fire, feed, feed!

Sick as hell, we fill our cavities with empty vows
vowels bawling in wilful abandon
vulgar fricatives and sibilants cursing angels
unwieldy wildlings burst to bear fruit
all over, over and over again

Between two lovers waging yet another war
lies the heart of it all, crashing.

FATHERDOM

All rise!

All ye volunteers new

Gather ye bodies and erect ye barricade

Prepare to face the threat, each of ye

Stand proud, stand prouder, stand proudest

Ye are the multitude, ye are wildfire

Ye will collect pearls from the orient seas

To fill ye chest, to fuel ye hearth

All ye volunteers new

All rise!

> O mighty Fatherdom, grant us thy mercy
> deliver our souls from the floods of hell
> we pledge our piety, we plead for plenty
> we rise as a nation, we protect one for all!

Proud are ye who stands in my presence

Ye shall be rewarded with a man-made island

Hundreds of nautical miles away from our foe

Prouder are ye who stands in my presence

Ye shall be adorned with three medallions of war

And billions of bullion coins to line your path

Proudest are ye who stands in my presence

Ye shall be granted acquittal without a doubt

The people will forget when history rewrites

All rise!

> One nation rises, bygone dynasties fall
> we pledge our fealty, we plead for family
> deliver their souls from the floods of hell
> O mighty Fatherdom, grant us thy mercy!

PROGNOSIS

2:12 pm, observe the mumbling of his lips

7:38 pm, monitor the pulsing veins under his collar and cufflink

3:44 am, record the rate of spitting curses oozing out of his pores

He is not my patient, but I must take very good care of him
especially his most honourable name

progeny		family	gene	
	crest		phylum	pedigree
spawn		genus		
dynasty	blood		offspring	
breed		class	kin	
specie	clan			seed

proof of his tremendous virility

Should he ask for a kiss, what else can I offer but my thirsting lips?
Let him rip my willing bosom apart, if only to feed him my heart,
until he regains his vigour, my Hippocratic oath fulfilled!

Whilst still tonguing his most delectable name,
I steady my hands to sign another medical opinion
and prepare for an important announcement by early light
enough to silence naysayers and newsmakers

6:06 am, long live!

DAY 26, UNTAMED VANITY

He stands proud
blinded in front of a gasping crowd
palms facing his burning eyes
fingers dancing, groping his hair
feet prancing, lifting his voice
soul gyrating, evading the shackles
thrusting
into the mob

He leads a chorus of bewilderment
and relishes their innocent tongues
savoury mush

> They conjure wilful acts of suicide
> concealed in sheaths of seduction
> their palms, stained with blood, gesture wildly
> their numbed fingers restrict their reach
> their feet, engraved with bruises, twinge madly
> their blinded souls force and release their grips

Beyond the rhythm
his music seduces incessantly
hips and limbs mustering another move
beat after beat, carnage after carnage
a display of affection for his murderous beasts

> their unrestrained spirits ever still unwavering
> their eyes, lifted in orgasmic highs, grimace plainly
> their wooing voices compel their brazen egos
> as they leapfrog into the beating night
> without meeting the face of light.

BOARDING

Eight crashes in less than a month, fuelling cockfights.

The fire lingers. The fleeing rages on.

A scholar was supposed to return to her lover's arms, this month,
I was told. But she had to patiently wait, she was bold.

> Your mother tongue on the scanner, please
> refrain from smiling, remove your cheap coat
> attention, look here, where are you headed to?

Another doctor was planning to leave for a better place, so I heard.
No, she was prevented by rules and regulations changing, of course.
She once adored the same person who rewrote the letter of the law.

> Present your pass when you reach the border
> a well written proof of your duty and devotion
> your new assignment is to eat your words!

Two decorated soldiers were granted four months leave to return
to their expecting wives. Said their superior in the 6 o'clock news.
Instead the two had to remain and man the far-flung outpost as
unexpected platoons of rival forces stepped in.

> Salute or surrender, you inferior troopers
> have you no maths to count distances and dashes,
> who gave you permission to spread your seed?

Behold the migration of sitting ducks.

One of them is it.

TERMS OF CONTRACT

Halved by their next of kin, indivisible by virtue
two lovers were annulled by the border wall

Witnesseth:

The North lies, north of the South,
the South lays down another demand.

The North lies, west of the South,
the South lays down another armband.

The North lies, centre of the South,
the South lays down another heartland.

The North lies, east of the South,
the Southeast and the East lay down their dead.

> Witness:

> They are closing in
> unless you flee the hell they are

Pen your name here, sign our deal with a kiss.

> I hereby declare the truth and nothing but
> under penalty of perjury, sabotage, and treason
> binding my oath for all intents and purposes
> pursuant to the vow of my lawfully wedded
> sign my name, cross my heart
> hope to die.

DEADLIEST DEADLINE

Haven't you heard
Fatherdom has conscripted his gatekeepers?

Did they not fight for
~~prevention~~ ~~people~~ ~~privacy~~ ~~power~~ ~~pragmatism~~
~~posterity~~ ~~protection~~ ~~possession~~ ~~peace~~ ~~parity~~
~~prosperity~~ ~~populism~~
principle?

No, their fights are merely for payback.

Haven't you heard
Fatherdom was responsible for their deaths?

Did they not die of
~~pestilence~~ ~~punishment~~ ~~pessimism~~ ~~prison~~ ~~penance~~
~~prodding~~ ~~probity~~ ~~poisoning~~ ~~predators~~ ~~pomp~~
~~passion~~ ~~protest~~
patriotism?

No, their deaths are merely for profit.

OFF! OFF! OFF! OFF!

Rogue readers turned him off, off, off, off
Parody peddlers turned him off, off, off
Obedient orators turned him off, off, off
Authors, historians, journalists
turned a blind eye

> Memorise their badges, faces, names
> they will clean up this shithole of a mess
> they will come back for more
> control your devices as they come

They are closing in
unless you flee the hell they are
burn your bridges, cremate your idols
but never forget his unholy face

> Infectious breaths fill the atmosphere
> fourteen million fornicators at hand
> sixteen million fanatics rising
> seventeen million felons at large
> fifty-seven million faddists strong
> sixty-two million frontliners to spare
> eighty-five million fucktards galore
> ninety-one million filibusters wild
> two hundred million faithfuls combined

Fatherdom, have mercy on thy kindred
deliver our souls from the fires of salvation

hear our prayer   Off! Off! Off! Off!

our pledge   Off! Off! Off! Off!

our plea   Off! Off! Off! Off!

In the Southeast lies a province of great importance to Fatherdom:

teeming with seawater
(almost enough to quench the thirst of his pride)

surging in salesfodder
(almost enough to fill the depths of his greed)

reeking of manpower
(but not quite enough to die for the object of his lust)

Three months have passed since and the borders remain wide open, never mind the undead already marching the earth. And in spite of the swelling clamour outside, the personal chamber orchestra of Fatherdom conjures eerie pacific sounds.

AN ANTHEM ANATHEMA TO ETHOS

How could we listen to this gibberish?

HELD HASHTAG

Call it #viral with a hashtag.
Then describe how it exploits and perpetuates inequalities.
Like a pandemic breach of the peace among us.

Spread a #virus with a hashtag.
Now inject some humour and infect our bodies instantly.
Like a pandemic breach of trust between you and me.

DAY 99, LIBERTY AT LAST

Staccato.

Red clouds hovered upon the seamless sky
gleaming arrows rained and sprinted
like fireballs and staggering beams
countless roars, cries, bellows and screams
blended into a chorus of ceaseless grief
heroes and warriors and fearless soldiers
trampled the earth in their dreadful flight
their shields and rusted swords rattled
banners and pennants undulated
with life and death, and life after death.

> Beyond the rhythmic gasps
> the silence seduces incessantly
> each corpse mustering another move
> fleet after fleet, carriage after carriage
> a final act of undying devotion

And I?

I kissed the rumbling ground
sealed my lips, with dust, soil and mud
dug the earth with my numbed hands
waited for the unrest to commit suicide
and I prayed for silence to conquer the land.

> I pray that you pray that I pray
> unless you flee the hell they are closing in

And as the last arrow flung itself across the sky
before my eyes dimmed and my soul lost grip
I saw your face and loved you for the last time.

PART II
COUNTER CURFEW

LOUDSPEAKER

Many have succumbed
announced the loudspeaker:

You who are left standing be forewarned

Fall into line
Pay your dues and taxes
Count your blessings

> Sounds like a harmless order, don't you think?
> An innocuous attempt to say grace, save face
> when we are at the brink of brimming, breaking
> our bodies, hearts, lungs, spirits on the line

Count your blessings, you fools!
Stop complaining, you all stay put!

> Unless you flee the hell they are closing in

Many have succumbed, didn't you hear?
So, lock your traps up, or out you go!

> Out cold we go, why don't we spell that out.
> Despite what the curves and numbers say,
> they are not nameless figures or silhouettes
> but their names shall serve no purpose at all
> if we simply fall into line, pay dues, pay taxes
> count our blessings, we fools.

DAY 145, NEMESIS

Your vision
captures hues, grains and textures
reveals distorted compositions and disturbing montages.

> This is the recorded footage of the incident:
> the dominant beast is perched on a dying body
> seconds now, the beast will feast on its kill

The thin film at the surface of your eyes
is parched
and the thirsting soul beneath your pale skin
envies the seemingly endless watery streams
that flow in your mind

> Another recording of the same incident plays:
> the asphyxiated body uses its remaining energy
> to bellow a deafening sound, alerting the wild

Whilst you sleep,
your body awakens vivid dreams and mysterious stigmas
your innermost desires melt into purées of colours

> Herds of beef are closing in
> unless you flee the hell they are coming for you
> they come in droves, vengeful rank and file

reds, scarlet and crimson
blues, cobalt and indigo
yellows, greys
and jet black

> They are closing in
> unless you flee the hell they care

One day, you shall glare
at the bloody bludgeoned sunburst
crushing concrete and plastic skyscrapers
blistered eyes, unrecognisable faces, mutated beasts
your reflection in the mirror

> Watch the playback,
> you might have missed it.

You will see me, and we shall try again.

BLAST

She looks outside the window
as her aged, tender hands
glide past glass, metal, wood, water, air
in seemingly endless circular movements

She repeatedly gestures mental notes on each surface and texture
hands holding on for dear life, memories of her dearly beloved husband
and two, three children who never fail to greet her on special occasions

Today is one.

She pauses and smiles
the same way she did
for the past twenty years back home
in front of an obligatory camera

One flash, here comes the shock

But she is far gone now to witness the big reveal.

OLYMPIC SUFFERINGS

I want to say a few words
and pay some respect
to our bodies

as we commemorate
wars and truces
love games and massive fall-outs
victories and losses
mutual aids and benefits
vested interests and powers

I want to break the biggest chain
and provoke competition
to generate flak

as we consummate
affairs and romances
divine tragedies and dark comedies
dogmas and ideologies
worldly views and philosophies
vicarious salvation and bliss

I want to demand equal opportunities
and pay homage, less tribute
to our debts

as we conquer
suffering,
winning,
trying
everything
within reach.

LE TERRORISME TUE LA CRÉATIVITÉ

C'EST TOUT SIMPLEMENT IMPOSSIBLE

CAR NOUS SOMMES TOUS DES ARTISTES

DEATH OF MEMORY

The mysterious darkness behind you
transforms into a wall concealing your body
from unwarranted gazes and curious eyes.

The empty stage reveals your illuminated flesh
you neither move nor open your jaded eyes,
and I fear most that I shall be too late
to save you from your ill fate
from your pen's blade and your stranger's hatred.

The frozen tips of your fingers timidly touch
the cold, deadened face of the floor,
and your lips — ah, those lips that only I love!
I can ever kiss no more.

Staring at a blank screen, my window, I imagine passers-by look up, their palms shielding their eyes against frequent sunbursts. This summer is the hottest by far.

One catches my gaze.

> *What should I do? Heart, pay attention.*
>
> *Get your pen. And a paper.*
>
> *Can't I use my phone instead, take a picture?*
>
> *Use your phone, but you must type.*
> *Quick, you don't have enough time.*

Another stops by. Looks me in the eye. And another. Grimaces and threatens to break in. More and more gather, I can hardly catch up so I keep squinting to recognise every one of them. And keep my mental notes as vivid as possible because I cannot type any faster. I am sure the crowd will leave the moment my eyes blink. I cannot let that happen.

> *Have you got all of them?*
>
> *I think so.*
>
> *Now, it's time to say your piece.*
>
> *I know.*

I have encountered times like these, as many others have too, when pressing *Send* proved to be the most heartless.

DAY 217, MOVE!

Sometimes, people do not see.
At times, they do not move.
They tend to ignore and stand still
without knowing what moves.

Like today —
We've seen people without eyes, without hands
we've seen some who choose to whisper
and we know they couldn't hear as well.

We walk and run and move about
and see countless faces and facelessness
garbled sounds and white noise piercing ears
forcing us to look.

>Move, please, move!
>Sounds like a harmless order, don't you think?
>We can see you from where you stand!
>Despite the curves and numbers rising, reeling
>nothing adds up in this madness.

Move, please, move!
Our innards are exposed, exhausted!
We have the right to demand what we need —
we need to know, we need to feel.

>From a single pinprick in the midst of the void
>faster than heartbeats rushing into the wild
>spread tongues of fire savouring its kill
>there's no chance of escaping.

Sometimes, people do not see.
At times, they do not move.
They tend to ignore and stand still
without knowing what moves.

SONS OF FATHERDOM

All rise!

                  Hush, the silence enunciates

All ye volunteers new
Gather ye bodies and erect ye barricade

                  Who can stand this
                  an anthem anathema to ethos

Prepare to face the threat, each of ye
Stand proud, stand prouder, stand proudest

                  They emanate bodily scents
                  danger tastes like rotten meat

Ye are the multitude, ye are wildfire
Ye will collect pearls from the orient seas

                  Bent and burned and at the stake
                  men harvest coal

To fill ye chest, to fuel ye hearth
All ye volunteers new

                  Saturn returns
                  year after year, tick after tick.

All rise!

HIGHNESS IS ALL YOURS

Does one have the patience
to lend one's ears to this subject
appearing, appealing before one?
Does one take heed?

What is one's pleasure
Your Majesty,
what shall this bold body bid?

Be it an arm or two, be it remorse,
be it told, be it done, be it now!
So long as one's delight be worth
one's time, one's gain.

Ivory towers and rhetoric aside,
this servant implores
one's merciful kiss, one's consolation
pray, deny this suffering heart the fear
of thy blazing sunlight, burning mane,
thine immaculate attire.

Pray, deny this humble vestiture
albeit sewn with stitches of moondust,
horsehair, orange peels, and merriment,
twigs, turnips, and mediocrity,
pray, refuse!

Your Highness is perfect.

UNPRECEDENTED

He turned rogue readers into authors

He turned parody peddlers into historians

He turned obedient orators into journalists

He turned a blind eye

If memory serves us right,
we are left to our own devices
smack bang in the midst of his mess

                    They are closing in
                    unless you flee the hell they are

Airwaves filled with vulgar madness
ninety-nine percent more contagious than spit
mouth fuming, mouth fumbling, mouth fucking
night after night, darkness after darkness
sons of bitches worship his ground zero

                    Return their gaze
                    grazing fire, fraying ground
                    pray, burn their sins to fuel the world
                    of timid beasts, trepid sods, torpid skies

Shield our mouths, noses, but never our eyes
dare leave this rotten territory if ever we must
burn our bridges, cremate our idols
but never forget his unholy face

Enough to upturn bodies in their graves.

INTERNMENT CAMPS

Six months in, the militarised lockdown still clasped our necks.
We were told that it was meant to keep us safe and warm
so we shield ourselves airtight, watch out for alms and arms.

>   They are closing in
>   unless you flee the hell they are
>   against the will of the free

Acres have burned
craters have erupted
count your blessings!

You fools.

KILL MY WORDS

Uncover
target lesions sound like move
can any more be denial intimacy

Recover
whose lips fluid make unjust
censor rule potent majesty

Undercover
neither know seal limbs
missing bodies lawless conspiracy

I don't want to use words,
homonyms, synonyms and antonyms

No, I refuse to make sense anymore
lest you use it against me
against my will
my freedom
of
expression

repression

suppression

oppression

omission

scission.

BEDTIME

Spaces are shaped by sound,
the ticking time allows me to see.
Eyes shut, I find many ways to sleep
but there's no way to silence my heartbeat.

Sounds shaped by spaces
the ticking of the clock lends me sight
but when I close my eyes to sleep
I find no way to silence my heartbeat.

Carve spaces out of silence,
time the ticking, wake the sleeping.
Exhausted, I turn another blind eye.
There goes my heart beating.

FIGURE No 14

White walls, white ceilings, white floors, white cube. Each surface unblemished, glossy glass panes occasionally reflect the warm halogen lights and silhouettes perched on pedestals. The myth of First Man and Woman, stripped of all earthly possessions, is rendered visible in three sculpted works: a marble resin trophy, a larger-than-life concrete replica, and a gilt plaster of Paris figurine. The archetypal imagery is reiterated — at the risk of becoming redundant — in three different parts of the spacious lobby, each time counter-poising the previous figure.

In the adjoining gallery, neatly stacked prints serve as souvenirs of lavish possessions, from Renaissance paintings to Regency-era silverware. Take as many as you wish — at your own risk of course, albeit no security camera will intervene — then leave the premises satisfied with your loot.

But first, before making an exit, behold a painting on an imposing panel papered over with a repeating pattern.

PART III
CITY OF ESCAPE

QUARTER PAST

Open the windows
and let the scarce summer wind
conjure figments and fragments
distant memories.

Remember how we were told to stay
indoors from March until May
only to let them in?

Dystopian mnemonics

It was already midday
when the sun woke me up
to voices, laughter, sounds familiar
playing in our living room.
The mirror gleamed by the foot of our stairs
as I raced my heartbeat down seeing myself
young at twelve
eight
two
thirty-seven and thirty-eight,
at last, we are complete!

Open the windows, I was told,
let our dissonant melodies wind summer back
and again.

Open the windows and leave
them be.

TWELVE HUNDRED MILES

Letters and characters deny me
your true song amidst this cityscape

My heart, where do I look?

Where else do I look,
when there are no more spaces to fill,
my heart, your story fills this place!

My heart, your story fills this place!

My heart, this place fills your story in!

How does your city's heart escape my senses?
Wherever I look, it is filled with songs
in various letters and characters.

litters and charlatans
lenses and cameras
lanterns and charades
locomotives and cars
liberals and celibates
literals and conservatives
lies and charms
levers and crates
libidos and compulsions
locals and centrists
letters and characters

They are closing in
unless you free this hell
dare deny yourself
of expression
repression
suppression
oppression
omission
scission

CITY LUNGS

Outside, the megacity is hastily recycling its fresh supply of oxygen. Is there really enough for each body and every one? Inside, I try to constrict my breath in short gulps, careful not to waste the rations of supposedly uncontaminated air.

> They are closing in
> unless you flee the hell they are
> against the will of the free

Since morning, I have been rummaging through the stacks of sentiments stashed away in my room. Perhaps many others are doing the very same thing. After all, we have been detained — whether we like it or not.

What else is left to do?

I recount.

DAY 219, MADMAN

Sometimes I hear the clock tick,
sometimes I don't.

Other times,
it ticks so loud,
louder than heartbeats rushing.
Whenever I'm alone
in a quiet room,
in a room other than my own,
in your room,
in a room other than your own,
I keep shutting out time,
I stare at the stark white walls
and those glossy glass panes that arrest
the solid state of our viscous words.

Haven't you noticed?
Time seems to unfold too slowly at the start,
at the very start where seconds stretch like minutes
and minutes stretch like hours,
but
towards the end,
it chases us like a mad unknown
to the finish line that we never actually reach.

> They are closing in
> unless you flee the hell I care

Before we run out of time and sand

> I know his face
> his lecherous countenance

if only for you, I shall never finish this piece

                but I dare never speak
                of his ungodly name

I'll offer you madly a heartbeat's skip

                take your poison
                words of his mouth

as if a single beat in time will never cease.

                against the will of the free

DAY 222, BURY THE DEAD

I witness another body
stripped off her mystic skin
exposed her flesh
bearing the brand of fraternity

She gasped secretly

    I know his face

    his lecherous countenance

    I deny my face of expression

specks of yearning seize her
by the collar

    whilst I purge him out of my system

heart raging with belting fury

    I shove his mouth with boulders of bodies

She claws through, pulsating flesh
morbid desires

    a single lick left him ruffled

This is not an act of desperation.
This is a test.

And, I tell you, I passed.

I finally severed you from my body.

And, at last, I revert to my pristine form
without any trace of you in my skin,
in my bloodstream,
    or in my heart

                my mind

                    my words

                            my past

                                my life.

HEY, YOU

Hey, look, it's you.

Look at those well-meaning eyes
looking through me, at me, just me.

Usually, no one notices (me)
usually, no one sends (me)
notes and cursive sentiments punctuated
with dots, ellipses, and unspoken thoughts.

And I used to wait
for hours and more,
just to follow your next bout and spree
crystal eyes, smouldering orbs, luminous rock
lingering mist, hissing rain, whispering fog.

I lock (myself in) my room and lock you out

I lock my(self) (in)doors and look (you) out

for notes and cursive words punctuated
with regret, acceptance, then finality.

Of all the chances in this world

(why) does one simply find another
(when) at this lonesome hour,
(where) in this (non-)place,
(what) on earth.

Hey, look, it is you.

TWO LAMPS

When two lamps dim,
much less hearts,
words, pictures, thoughts fade out
in spite of the moon, stars, lights
of glowing universes
and reveries.

In another life,
perhaps lamps and hearts light
neither reveries nor universes
but truths, starry or grim
in spite of two
glowing,
fading.

DAY 231, LOST AND FOUND

I will collect sensations
from simple tables and chairs, doors and windows
and empty boxes and brittle sticks of chalk,
turpentine, paintbrushes, and pencil cases.

> They are closing in
> unless we flee the hell who cares

I will collect sentiments and thoughts
from breadcrumbs and undelivered mail,
cups and pots, empty shelves and empty drawers,
faded blankets and tattered shoes.

> Whilst we rummage through
> rooms and rooms of likeminded sleepwalkers
> stuck in this middle classist towns
> we must count our blessings day by day
> we must collect coin after coin
> must we toss our bodies

All these I would do
to find you in every little thing, in every contraption
and books and records, maps, stars and dreams
because I sent you away, forgot about you
and I sadly miss you so much.

> Hunger is to love
> as pain is to privilege

Indeed, but what must I do
when faced with the guilt of a lover's passing?
It had to be me who had to turn her in.

AUGUST RAIN

When rain
eternally returns
do whisper, do not whimper
let her breathtaking downpour
inundate the senses, drench madness
engulf your every desire
mouth to mouth
resuscitate!

Revive!

Let nobody in

whilst you slumber deep

dipped in pigments, stained with streaks

of dyed dreams, insoluble sweat,

pray, hail the august rain

and cup your hands

when no one else,

nothing else,

holds.

IN PASSING

To write this part I don't just sit back

I sleep.

I throw my pen and paper
like I would fling about the covers and sheets
let the dreaming begin

it is where I will search for their traces or her scent

Where I would go back to prior days
in South Kensington
or alone in Southwark
or along Southbank
I would buy those nifty contraptions that twist around like mobiles
for babies' cribs and finally curl under the bed when it starts to snow.

Unlike in Hong Kong when it rains. Sham Shui Po, of all places.
People grip their umbrellas instead of mobile phones, a rare sight.
Now they lift their faces to look at wet they're going; you can finally
see them make faces and understand wet they do. Without this
weather smartphoning people can be so dry.

Unlike in Singapore when it drains, both the weather and the work.
As if jets of steam launch my mechanical desk to its full, unlimited
capacity, never mind if the team stays at Heng Mui Keng Terrace a
millisecond more after midnight.

Unlike in Manchester when it hails, everything halts.
Even the unbearable cold that cuts through thick layers of wool,
cotton, concrete, glass, and gladness.

Next stop.

When Florence sings, no matter if my mind hovers 33,000 feet above flat earth, her voice will haul my lungs back to Lambeth, 3:53 pm. Nothing is never too late.

I am well awake.

.... . .–.. .–.. ––– ... ––– ...

Beside me you sat and mindfully flirted with your iPhone:

I unsaw a photo of you, a dancer in all your naked glory, in black and white, the undulation of muscle, the pulsation of applause. Instead of fumbling or fluttering, my mind faced elsewhere. How you looked at me earlier knowing we did know each other only to brush the thought aside.

A mistake?
Can't a person change this much?

a familiar face
perhaps a fan you have never even met
seen one of your performances, early or recent
try harder, from Abelardo Hall to Cape Bojeador
Shall I remind you of your cruelty?

Never you mind.
Your fingers beware better
almost meeting and mirroring mine, twirling as they write
then you handed back my pen.

Never you mind.
Your eyes realise otherwise
almost weeping and barely lying, three blinks, just like that
their candid spark was gone.

HELLO, EVE

No evening is not a night of song
as soon as the clock's bow strikes the strings of my heart.

I shall hum the last few lines of our au revoir
before the exact tune escapes my senses
and your face, my sight!

I shall sing from chorus to coda, nocturne to aubade
to bridge the rest between us
never mind if ever I miss a bit of rhyme
as long as the unsung is finally said:

You will my body to sigh, you will my spirit to sing!

But we only have this night of song,
seconds of refrain,
endless soul.

Hear!

A symphony of tremolos surrounding your ears
a tenor from the deep, lathering your body with sea foam
billowing, bellowing, and blending
ocean arias and sonatas
atmosphere and sound
air and ground.

Hello, eve
expect the morning to whisk drops of dew into mist
distilling last night's high operatic madness
into a very act of selfish endearment,
a crime of passion, in other words
arrest me before dawn
tick, clock, tick!

FLOOD

You cannot sing

your breath is gushing with water

your lungs are pumping gasps instead of gas

TONIGHT, WE DIE

Tonight, we die

drowning in a sea of unanswered prayers

pitiless skies, implacable depths

selfish dawn.

REFILL

Chest-deep waters
challenge the heart and lungs
air numbed

Withstand the tumult
of ninety-four million drops of water
arrest this rapacious assault on land and sea
arrest that body! Arrest!

When
herds of prayers harvest not one grain
hoards of barrels not one saved for one prayer
not one dry, not one full, not one saved
under thunders and distress
utter more pleas, urge the merciless sky
placate this clamour, pacify this mob
appease the pilgrimage of souls
quench their thirst and surrender
give up
forever.

WASTELAND

Had I known you were left in the midst of the wasteland
I would have fled to be with you right then and there

Despite what threatens between the two of us
land-grabbed territories and disputed seas
false promises, debt traps, missing antibodies

I would have kissed you back, again and again

If only I still had a pumping heart.

THE FOUNTAIN

Remember
the final hours of our bloody fantasy
the closing words of our gory speeches
and the very last time our yearning eyes met
remember the pain
the dark side of our sorrow
the feeble sound of our anguish
and the very first time our longing lips met
remember the twists of fate
and turns we took
to impress, to please
to rouse, to waken
to comfort, to mend
to kiss
to miss
to bliss.

I want to burst
and release the spirit of you
from the grips and chambers of my heart
from the gory innards of my desires
from the bosoms of my memory
like a fountain,
of water, tears,
sweat,
and blood.

IN YOUR ROOM, SECRETS LIE.

IN YOUR BED THEY COME ALIVE.

IN YOUR MIND THEY ARE RELISHED.

Waking up from this flurry of a nightmare, I gobble up gallons of air to revive my consciousness. I must have left the window unbuckled. The unwelcome monsoon had blasted the curtains in my slumber.

By the time I reached dry ground, the city was already drenched in radio silence.

Fatherdom has ordered all screens shut down.

Save for my window.

PART IV
TERMINUS

RAIN OF LIGHT

Light
does not diminish when it rains,
where it floods, florescence unfolds
waterlilies, songs, prayers
heart, spirit, life.

Each drop whisking
into minute crystals of colours —
rubies, amber and citrine
emeralds and sapphires
lapis, amethyst, precious rain.

Incandescent, fluorescent, halogen
infrared, ultraviolet, gamma rays,
sunrays, moonbeams,
and stars
shall only dwindle when it rains
light no more.

RING-BOUND

Despite the golden calm in Singapore
and the late afternoon midsummer sun,
my fluttering, fleeting heart is flooding
as if the hovering typhoon in all of Manila
made landfall in Heng Mui Keng Terrace
and took over my pen, two, three blinks
the storm filled both my eyes, all ears!

Beating,
but the sound beats me.

Listen to the silver rain, ringing, roaring
and taking over one, two, three blinks
it's done.

How shall I recount, rewrite the past
three months under this thunderstorm?
Despite seas, oceans, or another shore?

Whilst on board, five hundred knots of clouds and words propel my train of thought into fresh (water, please) streams of (plain soda) consciousness ploughing the seamless atmosphere. Turbulent spasms arrest my heart.

At that very moment.

Despite the emotional rush that compels me to write in tongues, the distance that had accumulated in years tempered my perspective like glass.

Thus, I am ruining another page in my diary by not admitting an entry.

Instead, I reclined and pushed back brimming tears into canisters of suppressed spirit.

BARK

Sunny eyes and gleaming teeth
warm the still empty space in my room.
Even in the middle of the night
I hear the rumbling from his belly deep
almost mimicking the panting laughter
of a younger me

By the rhythm of his heavy breath
I could tell it's my window to sleep
not minding to see the languid sun
yet another day

Through the years, he saw my heart
wax and wane, we grew day by day
until somebody else swept me away
whilst he slept alone, just waiting
guarding my very room the only way
he knew how to wait for me

This year, I did come home to stay
rounded my whole world with you
almost fulfilling our brotherly bond:
you would never have to wait for me
ever again.

20TH DECEMBER

Son of Fatherdom,
protect thy child.

Son,
protect thy mother.

Love thy neighbour
pray, protect thy child.

ARIYA'S LIST

Geoffried, Sérci, Oalder Frae, Mereen
Trant, Thighuin Lannistre, The Red
Woman, Bérik Downdareon, Thoroughs
Of Meer, Eellyan Peyne, The Mountain,
Moka Úzon, Zassot, Gaddon, Feyrguzon,
Araúho, MacConel, The Lance Corporal,
Hankynson, Mattynglee, Aleksander,
The Plagiariser, The Defeated Candidate
for Vice President, The Three Percenter,
Yæp, Vicerral, Gonzoga, Calyda, Dyzon,
Zinas, Batto, Décastro, The Mærcos
Apologist, The Spox, The Other Spox,
The Master of Public Health, The News
Anchor, Jiulianni, The Singer, Villavicenço,
The Septuagenarian, Courbin, Chauvinn,
Kooeng, Layne, Thaow, The Retired Chief
Magistrate, The Faith Leader, The New
Appointee, The Speaker of the House,
The Octogenarian, The Nonagenarian,
The Secretary of Health, The Grouper,
Nuesca, Lourensana, The Ex-President,
The Chief Executive, Coomings, Fyuchs,
Zucherbyrg, The Foreign Secretary, Mr
Action Man, The Boxing Champ, Caietano,
The Other Caietano, The Appointed Son,
The House Deputy Speaker, The First
Female Speaker, The King, Proud Boy,
The Oath Keeper, The Davaw Death
Supporter, Bulsunaru, Putyn, Lamm,
Hooa, Xee, Tramp, The Other Tramp,
Aymee, Bon Goh, The 16th President.

WITHOUT DUE RESPECT

Not your puppet
not my master
no strings attached.

Ghosting you
is the only way
for me to haunt your mind
for the rest of your life
for as long as your brain
can pack grey mush
mishmash of memories
and matters worse.

You and your spineless puppeteers,
masterminds of unceremonious executions,
deny your lists of names and summaries of crimes
beyond the shapeshifting shadows of doubters,
trappings of revenants reveal your grotesque past
your ego, delusions, pretence and vanity!

May you rot not in hell but in the eyes of the living
for even the most vainglorious of demons
deny you out of spite:

not their puppet

not your masters

nothing is unwatched

NOTE TO SHELF

But you couldn't even read my mind
even if I were an open book, so to speak,
a conduit for expletives and clichés
if I were only, truly, as you imagined

For a split second there you had me
thinking about the person I used to be
tracing papers stacked like glass
a keeper of mental notes and breaks

Even before, beneath, or behind
this opaqueness there once was I:
self-made, then un-made, then un-self.

But for now, here I am simply holding
a hardbound book, saddle-stitched,
whilst cursing another back to the shelf

Still, you couldn't even read my mind
even if I were to close this chapter,
so to speak.

Hi
What you up to tonight?

           ...

      Sorry, just saw this, I was busy last night

Are you safe?

         What do you mean

...

Nothing. Just checking.

            Okay
     I can't go back home yet, this lockdown is
     eating up my savings would you believe??

...

Was thinking of you yesterday.
Worried about you.

          mmkay

           ...

...

        Hey, go sleep
    I know it's way past midnight there

Can't go on like this.

        What do you mean??

Nothing. Just checking.

···

Just checking??

You okay? Are you safe?

···

Safe, yeah, savings, no
What do you need to know

Nothing.

···

They are sending me to the frontlines
tomorrow

What??
What frontlines??

···

Hey, what do you mean??

They are closing in

What?? Who's they??

unless you flee

···

the hell I care

Wait
Lemme call you

A SONG FOR XĪ HÚ

Along the banks and bends of Xī Hú,
the west lake of heavenly Hangzhou
I sit, I sing, and sip sweet drops of mist
whilst the amber sun burned with rapture,
fiery arms, blazing embrace, feverish pitch.

Then, she seized my breath, the moon
a love long lost, I found just as soon
I sit, I sing, and sip sweet drops of mist
whilst my rubied heart ruptured in bliss,
arms aflame, emblazoned with your kiss.

Take me for a long walk along Xī Hú,
and light the fire in me, whilst I drown,
I sit, I sing, and sip sweet drops of mist.

Where have you been? Haven't you heard? The contagion is already breaking out in Central. She bolted the door as soon as her daughter stepped inside.

Anxiously, she rubbed her daughter's nose with a kiss of balm.

It is the least of our worries for now, Mama, her daughter inaudibly warned.

Dystopia has just started.

ODE TO PAPER

Once more, I write
on paper

once more, I acquaint myself
with an object so familiar
with my eyes, nose, lips, fingertips and ears
once more, I write on paper.

I remind myself
that it tears more easily
than the heart,
something so delicate that soaks too quickly
under a storm of tears
once more, a will
once more, I write.

I remind myself of my limitations:
a blank, finite space
cut and torn edges
one chance
and my propensity for ~~mistakes~~ errors

Again, I write.
~~blank spaces~~
~~infinite irrelevant stars,~~
~~obscure distant dreams.~~

Inch by inch,
stroke by stroke,
letter by letter my words bleed to their imminent death:
on paper they are fittingly memorialised
in my mind they never rest in peace.

EPILOGUE

An imminent truce between each lifetime awaits:

I no longer care,
I am afraid no more,
as long as I have your memory.

And, once, you had mine.

for all frontliners

who are risking their ~~health~~ lives

for our ~~lives~~ health

Part III : City of Escape

Part IV : Terminus

Photographs by Kristian Jeff Cortez Agustin

Locations: Brussels, Prague, Versailles, Manchester,
London, Roosta Puhkeküla, Tremblay-en-France,
Singapore, Liverpool, Manila, Hong Kong, Paris, Milan,
Hangzhou, Tromsø, Helsinki, Bangkok, and Lääne

KJCA

Since 2018, KJCA has been residing in Manchester, UK whilst conducting his research studies on photographing Southeast Asia at Manchester School of Art.

He is originally from Manila, Philippines, but has lived in Singapore (for a professional stint at the Asia-Europe Foundation or ASEF), Hong Kong (for his research work at Hong Kong Baptist University School of Communication/ Academy of Film), and London (for his master's degree in Visual Culture at the University of Westminster).

His artistic practice includes visual art (calligraphy, ink, watercolour), digital media (photography, film/video), performance art (movement, music, theatre, voice), and literature (poetry, songwriting). He often brings together these various specialisms into his curatorial practice and directorial experience — working in Manchester, London, Hong Kong, and Manila.

www.universeandwords.com

Printed in Great Britain
by Amazon